COSMIC ALLITERATIVE SONNETS

Ashraf A.

A book of alliterative sonnets.

ISBN: 9798589831658

SONNET BIG BANG

Brightest beginning before the total time,

A supreme singularity; sustained everything in existence,

Massive matters, every energy, and all of spacetime,

Even enormous entirety's four fundamental forces

As universally unified one, so stars still shine.

We're wandering in the dramatic darkness

But big bang ensuring an explosion; humans haven't seen

So spacetime spanning everywhere to enormous expanses,

Early entirety expanding so inflation is initiating;

Causing cosmic fluctuations flawlessly, everywhere in emptiness

Which will soon start cosmic crafting,

By faultlessly forming particles' plasma for purposes

Of forming fusion fuels with elementary elements within,

To form fearless shining stars that destroy darkness.

EXPANDING ENTIRETY

Explaining ever expanding, enormous entirety

In an arresting, alliterative sublime sonnet.

Honorable humans wondered; what's the actuality,

And where's our own world's cosmic coordinate,

But believed in a cosmic center by rejecting reality;

Before exploring earth's every colossal continent.

Truly, the earth exists in a gigantic galaxy,

orbiting around a special star; shining so great.

Our supermassive system is moving marvelously

with surrounding systems' similar speed rate,

always around a central cataclysmic supermassive singularity;

surrounded by an escapeless event horizon of dark death;

light longing to flee from that, fails fully.

So no cosmic center; cleverness can get!

GALACTIC GRANDNESS

How huge is ever expanding entirety;

Dreaming the design of galactic grandness!

Shining stars orbited by planets, persistently.

Galactic components are circumnavigating as always;

Around the central cataclysmic supermassive singularity.

So star systems are relatively restless;

Moreover, movements are governed by galactic gravity;

Worlds wonderfully wandering in void vastness.

Gorgeous galaxies are also assorted amazingly

As irregular, spiral, and elliptical classes.

So asking about an accelerating expanding entirety;

Dark energy, ensuring expansion of space

So gigantic galaxies are moving matchlessly

To dramatic distances, into the darkness.

UNIMAGINABLE UNIVERSE

Dreaming the design of expanding entirety;

In surrounding spacetime, shining stars,

Extreme energetic quasars, and every galaxy

Are always observed in observable universe;

Billions of light-years; equal to ninety-three.

That's this entirety's expanding expanse;

Rationally relative to whatever we scientifically see

But beyond that boundary, is dramatic darkness

Where cosmic creations are countless, so roaming relatively

In secretly spanning spacetime; their dramatic distance

Is so long that light with victorious velocity,

Is fully failing to exhibit their enormous existence,

To extraordinary earth's honorable humanity.

So there're things; we wouldn't witness ever.

MYSTERIOUS MATTER

Whatever we witness are average matter;

Making moons, perfect planets, asteroids, and

Gigantic galaxies of superbly shining star.

But colossal cosmos is gorgeously grand;

Complexly containing five percent of matter,

Twenty-five percent dark matter and,

Seventy percent dominating dark energy so greater;

Ensuring expansion of universe; we understand.

About all mysterious macrocosmic matter,

Marvelous minds must thoughtfully trend;

Then, why're we wondering later!

When fusion fuels entirely end,

Even enormous shining stars surely shatter

That turns them into infinitely dense, dark singularities.

COSMIC CREATION

The stars shining in deathless darkness,

Are elegantly explaining each cosmic creation;

In numbers, notable cosmic components are countless.

All asteroids and comets, have common composition,

They are amazing objects, orbiting in systems' space,

Smaller than the moons; in motion

Around profound planets and giants of gases;

Orbiting shining stars are fueled by fusion

Of hydrogen-helium in stellar shells,

And all occurring orbits are governed by gravitation.

So supersized stars are telling tales

about the profound phases of eventual evolution

of former dying dwarfs; turning themselves

into infinite, concealed curvature of secret spacetime.

COSMIC CONSTRUCTION

We're wondering about flawless formation

Of perfect planets and shining stars in systems.

Before the beginning of cosmic stellar creation,

Denser components of clouds; containing hydrogen gases,

Are centrally collapsing because of gravitation.

Then, they formed first protostars with process;

Known to all as active accretion.

All accretion, actively attracting matters' mess

To turn them into igniters of fusion,

That would win natural nuclear reactor race,

To become bright stable stars of perfection.

Main sequence stars are shining with grace,

Planets are forming with surrounding smaller accretion

Which would turn them into supermassive systems, soon.

REMARKABLE RELATIVITY

We're wandering within a colossal collection

Of shining stars, notably named galaxy;

Grandly governed by great gravitation;

Caused by curvature of spacetime, surely.

Moreover, mass causes that curvature creation

So surrounding macrocosmic matters fall freely,

To that curvature's center; causing concentration,

All elegantly explained in remarkable relativity.

We're wondering; what's galactic gravitation;

Causing comparably similar stellar speed, surprisingly!

Also causing complex curves of relative rotation

Of objects in galaxies, that the theories of gravity

Are failing to fathom so running to rejection,

That reassuring, the revolutionary mysterious dark matter.

STRANGE SINGULARITY

We're wondering; what's a strange singularity,

What's within it but can entities, ever escape!

What's its importance of existence in entirety,

What's its structure, stratification, or shape!

Is infinite internal information existing eternally,

What're the ways, it would basically behave!

So many mysteries but in rational reality,

Not an inch of information, clever humans could have

About anything of strange supreme singularity,

Or surrounding secrets of the confined cave;

Inside its escapeless event horizon's boundary.

So luminous light fully fails to ever escape

From there, that's rationalized in relativity

That says, singularity is spacetime's infinite curvature.

INESCAPABLE INFINITY

We're wondering about every entity's fate

If it travels, toward a huge black hole.

Assume, an astronomical matter's motion is set

So observing that object is our rational role.

That matter is moving superfast, straight

Toward a supermassive singularity's sole.

A black hole's gravity is grandly great

That triggers time dilation to all

So slows down surrounding time's rate

Relative to regions; having no black hole.

Even earth's environment and relative to that,

time surely slows down dramatically, with a whole.

As a relativistic result, that time could get

Dilation of longest length, to trillions of years.

FIERCE FIRE FLARE

We're wondering about the rare roar

Of shining stars; highly hotter as hells.

They're fierce fire flare, therefore

Their tremendous temperature yells

At the magnetic field to fearlessly bore

The strongly surrounding shielding shells

Of profound planets to design a door,

To tear the technological models;

Made of magnetic, electric fields' factor.

They're telling terrifying tells;

Truly, there's meaningfully more;

The magnetic field fearlessly hails

Highly hot flares, fight bravely before

Causing catastrophes to a cosmic civilization.

SONNET SUPERNOVA

We're wondering about superluminous supernova

Which is extremely energetic explosion

Thus temperature is hotter than the heaviest lava.

Every energy is electromagnetic emission

That traveling through the EM field forever

So light luminating cities of civilization.

But how brightest supreme supernovae occur!

Of course, collapse of cores, assures all action

That fully forces supersized stars to shatter;

Emits enormous energy's rush radiation

To enlighten expanding entirety's everywhere.

So stellar cores' could collapse for gravitation

If sustaining surrounding stellar structure

Is impossible, with flawless fusion.

COSMOS

Dreaming the design of enormous entirety;

Expanding everywhere, to all dark direction.

What a worthiest wonder; assorted artistically,

Even when every entity is in motion;

Managed brilliantly by greater gravity.

The complete cosmos is a complex collection

Of faultless filaments of gigantic galaxy.

Filaments are flawlessly adjoined, as attraction

Of dramatic dark matter's massive gravity,

Is holding huge galactic groups as assortation

And accelerating expansion is ensured by dark energy.

A filament is full of pixels as portion;

Each is gigantic galaxy, star sustaining entity

So a species should survive, with ethical evolution.

REMARKABLE REALM

We wondered about enormous entirety!

All matters arc made of small segments,

Together, they create cosmic enormous entity

Such as supersized stars and perfect planets.

We would wonder about atomic actuality,

Remarkable realms of small-scale particles,

Profound principle of universal uncertainty,

That managing mysterious worlds of waves

But beyond the grasp of general relativity.

Rationally, massless photon and matter particles,

show so strange wave-particle duality

In dramatic double-slit experiments;

Even proves that particles possess the property

Of wonderful waves, that's quantum mechanics.

STRANGE SUPERPOSITION

We're wondering about quantum mechanics,

Its uncertainty is utilizing strange superposition

In small-scale systems; sustaining subatomic

Particles; wandering as waves with perfection

Within all massive matters, even electronics.

Without solving any scientific solution

related to rationalized quantum mechanics,

Making modern machines is impossible for civilization.

In quantum systems, subatomic entities

emerge everywhere, ensures every position

but perfectly possess particular placements

whenever we make a meaningful observation,

that obeyed by every energy and all elements,

even elementary entities, such as Electron.

ELEMENTARY ENTITIES

Quantum Mechanics manifest particles' property,

Calculate circumstances, and all motion

Of matters; beyond big realms' relativity

And also all classical mechanics' calculation.

Scientific standard model, moreover meaningfully

Explains every small scale stratification,

All atomic and subatomic particles' property,

Which're witnessed in colossal colliders of hadron

That heavily accelerate atomic and subatomic entity

To examine every eventual, complex collusion

And also all aftermaths' actuality.

Quarks and leptons, are fundamental fermion

Thus they all are eternal elementary;

Making macrocosmic matters with certain combination.

MACROCOSMIC MEDIUM

We're wondering about macrocosmic medium;

Mainly made of surrounding spacetime;

Similar to flexible fabric so strange to some,

But has four fundamental dimensions; one time,

Three spatial, never separable so surely rum.

Every entity exists in surrounding spacetime;

When sun shines, light and life come

Celestially to the habitable home of humankind.

All always move in the macrocosmic medium;

Containing cosmic fields so keep in mind;

Matters manage to make mass; as continuum

When interact with the Higgs field; having kind

Of profound particles; known as Higgs Boson

But EM field ensures electromagnetic emission.

LARGEST LANIAKEA

The essential earth is moving marvelously

Around a special star, the sun so splendid.

Gas giants, plantless planets are outstandingly

Orbiting it, and also a big belt of asteroid.

Gigantic galaxies sustain shining stars,

Our own one is orbiting in mega Milky Way.

It contains countless but the universe

Is unimaginably infinite; in a relative way.

Wondering, what's holding huge galaxies!

Gravity, generating galactic group

But colossal cluster contains these;

Truly, that isn't the largest, nope.

There're tremendous, supermassive superclusters;

Such as Laniakea, the largest home of humankind.

SONNET SERIES, LEAF'S LOVE

A lonely leaf, longing for love

So smelling a flower's fragrance.

She smells like a lovely dancing dove,

Looks like a crown; cute but careless.

Wishing to have her but that's tough,

Trying to express emotion so easeless!

But beloved, how a heart could give up

When young you, is a gorgeous grace?

Hello, helpless is a leaf for love

So accept all affection, my mistress!

Hey, how hilarious; making me laugh!

In this tall tree, a petal princess,

That's truly magnificent me, so give up.

Why not witness; I'm forever flawless!

FLAWLESS FLOWER

Forever flawless flower, I amazingly am

but a lousy leaf is so cuteless, common.

Love, couldn't laugh so why you came!

Flower for flower; makes meaning, moron.

A leaf longing love, sustains no shame;

His helpless heart's refusing to go on.

In this tree, all average I am so no fame

but beloved, I am also long lone.

Hearts are hopeless; always try to tame,

Lonely leaves are countless; come on.

My heavenly highness, heartbeats are always lame

So sad soul's searching for that tearless throne.

There, the queen in a green realm

Is youthful you; heart has surely shown.

LOUSY LEAF

That's what, I'm trying to say;

I'm a queen in this tearless tree

But you are a loveless leaf so lousy;

remarkably rare is a flower; flawless as me

So go away, there's nothing to say.

Truly, I'm trying to make you see;

Love fails forever, to flee away

But youthful you, so long lasting, lovely!

So please, perfect princess, you may

Let a leaf's love fall freely,

Accept all affection; I'm longing to lay.

In every garden, green leaves are lousy,

Countless, cuteless, and common as clay,

That grants flawless flowers' gorgeous rareness.

TALL TREES

Fairly fascinating are all tall trees

That they bloom beautiful flowers, so flawless

But beloved, every environment naturally needs

lonely lovely leaves' gorgeous greenness

so surely, each of leaves, always gives

essential energy; ensuring all aliveness

and also assures perfect purities.

A leaf is lonely but we aren't worthless,

even every tall tree in taken territories,

is common but cause celestial cleanliness

to atmosphere around, and above all priorities,

provide peace in entire earth's environments.

After all, plants, leaves, flowers, and trees,

even every earthly entity's equal for eternity.

LOVE AT LAST

The flawless flower is falling in love;

She's so shy to say, so that's true.

My perfect petals might make their move

When winds touch them while traveling through.

See the splendid sky, all above;

Colossal clouds are crying to continue

This tremendous rain, to remove

Internal impurities so undeniably undue,

And all affection, I may approve

but if a lousy leaf turns truly into

A perfect petal that might move.

But beloved, it's impossible, no argue;

Always true is this limitless love

Thus this leaf, can become a petal for you.

NASTIEST NEXT

Days are diving into dreams,

Moments are moving toward memories,

Love of that leaf, the flower forever feels;

Truly, they're doing delightful deeds.

The leaf is turning yellowish

Thus yelling; where're my wills

But beloved, true love is

Giving this leaf a petal's kiss!

No, your youth is fading, foolish;

Oh, I am also drying; what's this!

Pure rain is now, this tree needs;

Lost is love when your youth perish.

But beloved, this leaf's love is truest

That can't change; careless of all nastiest next.

EXCESSIVE ENJOYMENT!

While enjoying all earthly wealth,

We're walking a worthless way,

To sight the shining sun.

Crying clouds are colorless clay,

Winds without wings having no fun.

What would the tortured sky say?

Can clouds and atmosphere, take the turn

By themselves, but how could they!

Where's the dramatic day of marvelous may,

Why wonderful world's on restless run?

What would these pathetic pollutions say,

To the worthless words; governed by glorious gun!

What would forthcoming future lay,

To the celestial children of honorable humankind?

FOREVER FREEDOM

Forever freedom is the truest destiny

So this rage, is roaming within me.

Where anger could take us;

Not even the eyes, ever dare to see.

Even love of heart can pass,

If fierce fury flows for eternity.

Even shining souls could collapse,

When outrage takes over each tree.

How we observe the uncertain universe,

Is how humanity, learns to live free.

Witness wonderful worlds of shining stars;

Wandering within ever expanding entirety.

A habitable home could cause a curse

When oceans and forests, lose all lovely purities.

SPIRITUAL SELF

Am I truly talking to you?

Maybe, I'm the one, who isn't;

Thy spiritual self's talking through!

Worthy words are dramatic depressant,

They wander within, without a clue.

Remarkable readers are embarking existent;

Into wonderful worlds which're wisely true.

The delusional one who's ever ignorant,

never reads to be free, nor can see

so fails to flee, from all unethical undue.

So saying surely; see the expanding entirety,

To gain knowledge that isn't for a few.

Wisdom's the obscure ocean's ethical eternity;

Freedom's a sailless ship there, thus be its cosmic crew.

THE FIRST ONE

My only, breathtakingly beautiful baby,

You're the truest perfect princess.

My only, fabulous freedom fairy,

Your exquisite elegance, is forever flawless.

My helpless heart's enchanting empress of beauty,

Your countless charms contain cuteness.

My matchless bonded beloved, you're perfectly pretty;

Your amazing angelic attractiveness is endless.

My splendid soulmate of every eternity,

My soul seeks your long lasting loveliness.

My heavenly heartmate of every expanding entirety,

Without yours, my heart is hopeless.

My sweetheart Sunshine of limitless luminosity,

Without you, I'm pathless, purposeless, as always.

WORTHY WOMEN

Worthy women are equally honorable humans;

Within a world, we roam rightfully.

Rejecting a faultless fact is ignorance,

We possess perfect rights, righteously;

Refusing to accept any, is arrogance.

Ethical evolution ensures progression, perfectly;

Failing to fathom freedom, is foolishness.

They give birth, raise blameless baby;

without women, future falls into darkness,

Between babies, prove ignorant inequality,

Between souls, show the delusional difference.

Between beats of human hearts, exist equality

But beats' stopping, shatter equal existence

So survive equally as ethical entities, of humankind.

TIME TRAVEL

Are you long lost but where?

To you, am I trying to travel?

Whoever writing words, isn't a liar;

Worthy wonderful worlds; we do unravel,

With writing, we ignited freedom's fire.

Let's travel to the time of caravel,

Amusements and drama of deadly dare;

Poetic people, were within hollow hovel

but of happiness, they loved to care,

They wondered with wisdom of novel;

True love and friendship, were there.

Nowadays, what're we digging with social shovel;

The tearful greedy graves, of poetic peace

that ensures heavenly ease, to humankind.

Bonus Pieces of Poetry

Dying Dreams

Wherever life goes;
Even the time,
As always follows.
When a soul shine,
Where the heart shows,
That's thy destiny,
A sight of souls.
Each is ethereal entity;
In the heartbeats,
Its spirituality flows.
Dream of eternity,
That's the truest grandness
Of the greatest goals.
Whoever afraid of darkness,
Greets the dying dreams
So go beyond your fear.
Let not your dream die
But let thy soul hear
That the heart, can't tell a lie;
even its soul has an ear
that can hear, the screams
of those dying dreams.
Remember my dear,
that soul of yours,
always remains younger
so keep pursuing thy dream
to never become older.
Or you would die, with burdens
on thy soul's shoulder
that crying for the crime
of destroying the dream
that could have kept you younger;
even at the breaths' end.

Ashraf A.

Worthy Writing

Wah, what an amazing art;

Coming from the celestial core,

Of your heavenly heart!

Forever freedom!

That's the perfection of poetry;

Emerging from a sovereign soul's

Pleasant prosperity!

Worthy writers!

We benefit humanity,

With wonderful words;

Wandering within worlds.

Ages to ages, soul to soul,

Every word passes.

Time to time,

Words are arriving as waves,

Raining as rhymes

From the beginning of humankind.

-!- AA -!-

Made in United States
North Haven, CT
21 February 2022

16303685R00022